# Watch Your Head 2

poems & plays by

# Kevin Rabas

Kellogg Press    Topeka, KS

Also by Kevin Rabas

## POEMS
*Bird's Horn*
*Lisa's Flying Electric Piano*
*Sonny Kenner's Red Guitar*
*All That Jazz*
*Everyone Just Wants to Drum*
*Watch Your Head*
*On Drums*

## POETRY CHAPBOOKS
*Eliot's Violin*
*Bird Book*

## POEMS & STORIES
*Songs for My Father*
*Late for Cymbal Line*
*Like Buddha-Calm Bird*

## SHORT STORY COLLECTION(S)
*Spider Face*

## NOVELS/NOVELLAS
*Green Bike (with Simmons & Graves)*
*Elizabeth's City*

Watch Your Head 2
Copyright © 2020 Kevin Rabas

Published by Kellogg Press
Topeka, KS
www.kelloggpress.com

Curtis Becker, Editor
www.curtisbeckerbooks.com

Please consider contacting the author at:
Kevin Rabas
PO Box 274
Emporia, KS 66801
or krabas3@yahoo.com
www.kevinrabas.com

All rights reserved. No part of this publication may be reproduced, distributed, or transmitted in any form or by any means, without prior written permission of the copyright holder.

Written permission is required for professional live performances of any of the plays in this book. This includes readings, cuttings, scenes, and excerpts. Additionally, anyone receiving permission to produce any of the plays in this book is required to give credit to the author as sole and exclusive author of the play on the title page of all programs distributed in connection with performances of the play and in all instances in which the title of the play appears for purposes of advertising or publicizing the play. Public performances of the plays contained in this book are subject to payment of royalties.

Printed in the United States of America

Eric Sonnakolb, Cover Design

Dave Leiker, Photography

ISBN: 978-0-578-70865-2

Library of Congress Control Number: 2020940442

# **Praise for** *Watch Your Head 2*

In *Watch Your Head 2*, Kevin Rabas offers more of his poetry of self care while recovering from a brain injury. Even as the poems are older, the reader can still trace back to how they are Kevin Rabas reflections on life, class, position: "I think of the men / I could have been— / if my mother had not / led me to the water's edge / of books." Also in this collection, Rabas shares his playwriting. Just as his poems reflect a Midwestern deep life, his plays do, too. His wit and charm shine, like in "Lemonade." While the conversation between a young man getting a haircut and the stylist turns to Jazz, she asks if Charlie Parker, Miles, Coltrane, Keith Jarrett are any good. His response: "Let me tell ya, they make Kenny G look like Fabio just holding a horn." As a long time Kevin Rabas fan, I love this rich volume of poems written two decades ago that still holds up today. If you are new to his writing, *Watch Your Head 2* is just a great introduction to it as any of his collected books.
 –Dennis Etzel Jr., *Everything is Ephemera*

Take a twenty-year step back — a transformative time for Kevin Rabas. Between a head injury, divorce, friends parting ways, and meeting the love of his life, these poems bring the reader through some of the deepest introspection and observation we have seen from Rabas yet. Some of these poems emanate a warm light and tickle of romance, bravery and confidence—the curiosities of young adulthood. Other poems are reminders that even when all seems lost, we can use our poetic voice to find the way home.
 –Linzi Garcia, *Thank You*

*for Lisa*

# Table of Contents

## Poems

| | |
|---|---|
| [littles] | 1 |
| [over recess, grade school] | 2 |
| [at the sandlot] | 3 |
| At the Auction | 4 |
| [modern pastoral, Luray, Kansas] | 6 |
| Working Class | 7 |
| [Bird borrowed my horn] | 8 |
| Scotty | 9 |
| Faerie Tales | 10 |
| Engagement Pralines; Bea Speaks | 11 |
| Bea | 13 |
| Air Heart | 14 |
| I Spend My Life | 15 |
| [rings] | 16 |
| [the foot] | 17 |
| [chickadee] | 18 |
| [forget soup spoons] | 19 |
| Artt Sketch | 20 |
| [blues] | 21 |
| [sidewalk cracks] | 22 |
| Athena, KC | 23 |
| [signatory] | 24 |
| [honeydew] | 25 |
| [underwater] | 26 |
| [before they admit me] | 28 |
| [urchin] | 29 |

| | |
|---|---|
| [Wednesday, 3/8/99, 11:50 p.m.] | 30 |
| [black bird] | 31 |
| [if you choose] | 32 |
| Mad John Speaks | 33 |
| My Own Marx | 34 |
| [hold] | 35 |
| [travelers] | 36 |
| I Call Out | 37 |
| [young lover] | 38 |
| Work Song | 39 |
| [charmed] | 40 |
| [new lease] | 41 |
| Lisa's Gig | 42 |
| [hold on] | 43 |
| [and like a clanging gong] | 44 |
| Arpeggios | 45 |
| [leaves] | 46 |
| Goatee | 47 |
| [designing Lisa] | 48 |
| [the taste of you] | 49 |
| [moving Lisa] | 50 |
| On the Road | 51 |
| Yellowstone Nature Sketches: A Sequence | 52 |
| [the sign of the rabbit] | 54 |
| [tea cups] | 55 |
| [note for Lisa] | 56 |
| [painting the walls together] | 57 |
| [painting the walls together #2] | 58 |
| Always, my love, you fill me | 59 |
| Isabelle | 60 |

The Neighbors                               61
[waiting for you]                           62

**Plays**

Lemonade                                    65
Elves                                       77
The Broken Cup                              91
Baby on a Plane                            101
Community Blood Bank                       113

# Introduction

I wrote these poems in 1999 and 2000, while I was going through a divorce and recovering from a head injury. (I was in a pick up basketball game and got knocked down.) I was also unemployed and living with my parents again.

With the help of Linzi Garcia, I excavated these poems and revised them. They have a kind of simple, raw power, so I wanted to share them with others.

This book also includes a handful of plays I wrote from 1996-2009. The plays seem to follow and speak to the themes and subjects of these poems. Also, they share many of the same characters. In terms of time, there is overlap with when many of the poems were written. They're from roughly the same period in my life. I hope you enjoy reading these plays, and I hope a few theatre companies take them on and produce them. (If I can, I will come watch.) These are my first plays.

It was curious revisiting this material, which is a sequel to my earlier book which covers some of this same ground, *Watch Your Head*. Many thanks to Curtis Becker, who selected, edited, and published both books.

These poems were written in Shawnee and Manhattan, Kansas, as well as in Kansas City; Plainfield, Vermont; Yonkers and New York City; and at Yellowstone National Park. I traveled about more back then. Was sometimes rootless.

–Kevin Rabas, 29 January 2020, 9 am, Emporia, Kansas

# Poems

## [littles]

In Yoshi's studio we found miniatures
of his finest sculptures: $25 each.
      My wife
      pours me tea
      for one.

I am a child again.

**[over recess, grade school]**

Pull harder, someone said,
and the boy held onto the bar
of the jungle gym while the mob
took hold of his legs
and pulled, stretched him.
I told him to let go, and he released
one hand and punched me in the face.

We became friends after that,
once my eye healed.

**[at the sandlot]**

I picked up a blue plastic shovel.
You held a red bucket. Together,
we began to dig.

## At the Auction

When one of their children returned home looking beaten, heartbroken, the Kellers took them the only sensible place—to the farmer's market or to the auction—believing that the world was still full. Fresh fruit could be bought for pocket change. Chickens could be bagged and brought home. An antique coffee table could be carried away for less than ten dollars.

My father, who works as a construction superintendent, donned a polar fleece jacket the color of money and ushered me into the auction hall.

"Follow me," he said, "and don't touch anything. Just look. Use this list." He handed me a list of the items up for auction. "And write down your bids for what you're interested in. Always bid low. And never go over the number you write. That just spells trouble."

At the entrance, we passed a table full of musical instruments: a greening trombone, an accordion with a bellows full of holes, a banjo with only two strings. Up front, the tables were full of knick knacks, glassware, place settings, tackle boxes, pipes, lanterns, rifles, pocket knives.

My father pawed through the tackle boxes, searching for old lures. An old man picked up a curved knife. Others dry-fired the guns, aiming at the wall where the affluent inspected golf clubs. I passed up the guns and golf clubs and settled near the pipes, lamps, and lanterns. Something with smoke, something with light. Somehow there must be a way to guide one's way. But can that be bought? Can that be sold?

## [modern pastoral, Luray, Kansas]

The dry earth is covered
in spent shotgun shells,
blossomed at one end;
shot pokes star holes in the sky.

The milo's up, and we can run in it again.
Behind us stretches the road sign for the Motel 6.
Farmers honk their tractors at us as they pass
on the long blacktop stretch into town.

Old women come with buckets full
    of cold pond water.
Old men arrive with logs on fire
    in their arms.
Stretch out & pull the clouds from the hilltop—
where the scout is buried, where
a mortar & pestle mark his head.
He watches for the ridges
on the horizon, the old buffalo
beyond the herd on what is now
my father's father's last small plot of land.

**Working Class**

I think of the men
   I could have been—
if my mother had not
led me to the water's edge
of books—without them
I would now rely
upon the strength
of my back, my hands—
instead of the scattered thoughts,
the flock of disparate birds
in my head.

## [Bird borrowed my horn]

The horn was mine, the notes
his, like the ragged tunes
of old men
hanging laundry
over the alley.

**Scotty**

Not long ago,
you wore only red Converse tennis shoes
behind the drumset,
your legs always pumping,
blood full of sugar,
eyes fully open,
your glasses often fogged
w/ the heat rising
from your face.
You grooved so far
into the subconscious
that sometimes you returned
from your trance
to a body convulsing
in a panic attack.
You knew Caesar's affliction,
Caesar's ambition, grace.
Scotty, I spent my life
in a practice room next to yours.
While mine rose in temperature,
yours was always on fire.
Oh, how you fanned the flames.
Oh, how you pitted your skins
against the best.

## Faerie Tales

Who knows why you let down your hair
for me? My arms were not made for climbing. I
will pull my way up, if I can. If I can't, you may
have to wait.

## Engagement Pralines; Bea Speaks

Your clothes were in my wash when I asked you
    to leave for the last time.
Together, we filled the slots of my apartment's
    great white machine with quarters
that summer when we returned
    from New Orleans.
I had never loved a man so long,
although the boys in my small town
said once one died for me.
They loaded his Impala with what was left:
summer sandals, two pairs of stone earrings,
    a summer dress,
a sweater, a toothbrush, and what I kept in
    a see-through bag
for nights spent in his bed, one spare pair
    of red, lace panties.
All of these the boys hung out the windows,
    dragging dirt-road Main,
and scattered on the sidewalks and the store
    fronts, my sandals
in the road. Later, under the black shawl
    of twilight, women
carried bundles of our life home. Charlene
    keeps my earrings
on her husband's mantle, a reminder, I have
    seen them, tokens
transitory as the glances and the kisses we offer
    for our lives.

Kevin Rabas

>One day Charlene may hand me back my own
>    ears' intimate, lost hooks,
>precious as the red box of pralines I now keep
>    beside my bed, your final gift.
>I know you reconsidered in New Orleans, after
>    the two-day-long
>drive from Kansas City in which we argued until
>we both spat out windows onto black road.
>When our hearts grew calm
>I heard you whisper what you truly wanted
>before our bodies grew cold, our mouths hot:
>the stones and gold the voodoo woman sold
>for a finger, or to hang upon a neck.

**Bea**

I remember when
we drank gin
beside your apartment pool.
You played the part
of Dorothy Parker.
Anyone could tell
you had decided
I was on my way
out. "Call me
when you're 30," you said.
"Maybe then we'll both be ready—
for rain, for bells, & rice."

Kevin Rabas

### Air Heart

Amelia, I never could have known you,
although this past week I visited your house,
read your marriage license, where
you'd crossed out the part
about "under God," and written:

*If it doesn't work after a year, honey*
*if we are not happy*
*we must split, fly.*

So much like birds.

Where did you land, my dear?
Heaven only knows.

## I Spend My Life

Although I know
I spend my life
more as a branch does
bowing to the wind,
rising and falling, waving,
the metronome's stick
ticking off time,
I wish I were a trunk,
rooted to the depths
of clay, sand, and rock—
to which I will return
when the wind is through
with me.

**[rings]**

She said, "I threw my ring in the river."
I still wear mine
hung 'round my neck.
Come back
and slip
it onto me.

**[the foot]**

I.
You held my head
in your hands tonight.
Someone could stop
the buzzing, put me
to sleep.

II.
I watched closely
the masseuse's feet
as she worked on the back
of my head, told her
she was better than
any drug, thanked her,
and her foot stamped
the carpet,
reminding me
where I was.

**[chickadee]**

I have lost
my little chickadee,
the woman who swung at me
once in the night, fist against
chest, until I held her
and cried and retreated to
the laundry room, a small hell.
I love her still, although
I have lost her.

**[forget soup spoons]**

I could eat my life
with a fork and steak knife.
Forget soup spoons.

## Artt Sketch

Artt held his arm
like a captured snake;
it twisted in his fingers.
A boxer knows
this struggle with the self
as much as the double trouble struggle
in the ring: its lights,
its mat, its man
with his red hands up,
and also those
writhing ropes,
when you are stuck,
cornered, pinned.

**[blues]**

Rise from the rocks
like saxifrage. Break me
with your song.

*ala "A Sort of Song" by William Carlos Williams

## [sidewalk cracks]

October rain
in the city.
Watch how the cracks
in the sidewalk
expand.

**Athena, KC**

She stands above our city,
black sword in hand,
the daughter Zeus bore
alone. She sprung
from his dreams, his head,
full of rage and war,
and with a beauty few who knew
war could resist. Athena,
judge of men, I know
when you look down
at these sidewalkers, these men
committed to towers and shops
with their briefcases and bright paper
bags with the looped rope handles
in hand, these men who have
not known the dark path
to battle, you must
either laugh or weep.

## [signatory]

Your signature no longer comes
with "Love," instead
"Sincerely" now—
at the end
of a summons.
How many times
must I testify
to my love?

**[honeydew]**

I rise without a shower
& go get groceries.
Across the parking lot
birds chirp
over the rhythm
the grocery cart makes,
a squeal & squeak
of rusted wheels.
Someone knows the words
to the song of spring,
and they're not telling.
In my cart the honeydew
ripens. In my mind
a blade dives deep
into the juice, parting
the white veins of age
and seasons past.

## [underwater]

I hear my heart in my head
underwater.
I come here to pray
underwater.
I put my feet flat on the tile wall, straddle
    the spigot, my eyes
underwater.
I count my breaths
underwater.
I slow them down until I am nearly asleep
underwater.
I hear the neighbors laboring, coughing, making
    love, here in HUD housing
underwater.

My wife moves the shotgun, drags the bed by one post, one leg, across hardwood floor, away from the whispers that come from our conservative neighbors, words through the wall, our headboards head to head. My wife takes off her clothes, reads me psalms, says I'm not yet ready again for her sex
underwater.

    I pack all the shotgun shells into a bag
        & cart them
    to my parents' home, fearing she will

use them
underwater.

I throw darts against the wall, call myself
      a mutt of 21 flavors
underwater.

I consider hacking my ring finger off
w/ a knife, w/ a hatchet
underwater.

I profane my own name, bang plates
      against cups
in patterns of the trinity
underwater.

I commune w/ Konza Prairie buffalo
and their young
underwater.

I check myself into Menninger's
underwater.
I leave my wife
underwater.
I leave my
I leave my

Kevin Rabas

## [before they admit me]

I take off my glasses.
I won't need them.
I'll see this world
with my own eyes,
whatever the blur.

**[urchin]**

This evening I feel as simple-hearted
as an urchin attached
to the bottom
of a shallow sea.

## [Wednesday, 3/8/99, 11:50 p.m.]

I know
your sins
are no worse
than mine.
I only ask now
for a little forgiveness.
I bow down,
my feet in the creek.

**[black bird]**

Black bird
leaps
from brown branches
into evening air.
Feathers
descend
onto lake skin.

Kevin Rabas

**[if you choose]**

If you choose,
the hills will
dance like lambs,
the mountains
like rams.

*Psalm 114: 4

## Mad John Speaks

I love the feel
of sanded wood.
I can see the river in it.

Hand me the hatchet,
& I will split
your sins in two.

## My Own Marx

I go down the stairs
from your apartment.
Outside my truck
waits. I will drive across
the city and into the suburbs
where my parents live.
Divorce has led me here.
Injury keeps me.
I will move just as soon
as I can. But will I
move in with you?
The streetlights all glow green.
My headlights burn orange
on the pavement
on the road home.
I know my way.

Every dollar earned
through Marx's market
brings me another spot of carpet.
I will not need to pawn my own coat
to find you at my door. My dear,
your pots and pans are safe.

Find me in the newsroom.
Find me at the other end.
Forward all my calls
back home.

**[hold]**

My hands hold
the steering wheel top.
My elbows touch the bottom.

Like a praying mantis,
or a fetus,
I drive.

**[travelers]**

We are like the mechanical men
depicted in ancient Mayan
diagrams, hewn in stone walls—
levers & gears at every angle,
and in the distance—stars.
We are the travelers
of time & space,
masters of the machine.
No one doubts this,
not even the watchmaker,
time kept
in a pocket.

## I Call Out

I call out to all the women I have ever known.
One must know my heart.
I have lost my wife, I say.
Did you know her?
I held her until I could
no longer tell her hand
from my own.

I take long walks in the park alone.
I watch the wild grasses move.
Gossip spreads through nations this way
and travels on to the next. The Czech president
has married an actress.

Kevin Rabas

### [young lover]

Young lover,
heed the beat
of your own heart
before the tick
tock of society's clock.
Today is ever tomorrow,
and tomorrow is forever lost.

**Work Song**

Eighteen years old
and you already know
the "Work Song,"
something you need
to gig in this city.

You carry your trombone
like a cased pool cue,
always ready to swing.
You know where and how
to find your own tone.
Blow! Purse your lips
as if you know just what
to say. And sing.
Your song is never far off.
Catch notes in the night air
and bring them through your bell
to the woman in the front row.

## [charmed]

The snake charmers
are out tonight
w/ their soprano saxes,
causing the heart
to rise in your chest,
your aorta, your veins
& arteries swaying,
swinging.

**[new lease]**

God, you have lent me my life again
as easily as a cloud passes through
the tops of trees and returns
to the sky. (May I use it for you.)

## Lisa's Gig

In this bar,
the candles all burn blue,
and your voice holds
the room. Ice cubes kiss,
and billiard balls pop
to your tune.
And I think that I have heard
the first cries of our
unborn daughters
in the cat calls
from the men
in the shadows
with sticks.

I have drunk from
other men's glasses, sipped
from other women's lips
the very taste of tomorrow
tonight.

**[hold on]**

I now grasp a knob
as if it were your wrist.

Kevin Rabas

## [and like a clanging gong*]

Love is both the blossom and the bud.

Love is both the cymbal and the silence.

*1 Corinthians 13:1

**Arpeggios**

I rest in your bed.
You hold
the guitar.
The pattern you play
reminds me
of the webbing
of cat's cradle, your notes
so simple, the intervals
so close
I could dial them
on the phone.

**[leaves]**

I will hold you
like roots
hold a tree.
Honey, let out
your leaves.

**Goatee**

My chin now
grows the spines
of the cactus.
Like the cholla,
my mouth
is ready
to spring
& attach
to you.

*cholla: springing cactus*

## [designing Lisa]

I knew I loved you
when I saw how you
kept your plaza apartment,
w/ candles, antiques,
& fine rugs: things kept
up like an open piano,
all the strings and hammers
tight, arranged.

**[the taste of you]**

I hold you above
my tongue. Like
with Pavlov's dog,
ring in my hunger
for you.

Kevin Rabas

## [moving Lisa]

*I'll never move again,* she says.
I carry boxes into her new apartment.
*Forget moving in together.*
*You'll just have to move*
  *in with me.*

## On the Road

In the hotel
under this lamp,
I find the words
to describe your
muscular ballerina back,
your shoulders curved
as if carved in marble
or soap. We sleep late,
missing the maid,
& you make our bed,
reversing the bedspread
so it seems clean,
& I dream of the day
when we may have a house
& a bed of our own.

## Yellowstone Nature Sketches: A Sequence

The water's surface is
as still as
a plateau of drifting ice.
I dare not skip a rock.

Only wait and watch and a stool
will present itself, a rock you had
not yet considered a meditation seat.

My hottest breath creates a spectral cloud
that dissipates before I again inhale.

*Yellowstone Forest:*
Fire stops at the waterside, and on a hill
the tall grey dead overlook
their green peers below.

A trout breaks the surface,
jumping, arching so that he
hits his middle when he returns.

An osprey, holding a brook trout
in his talons, flaps overhead.

Everywhere there are insects,
weaving through
a windless evening.

*Spring Trout:*
If I had a dry fly,
I would lend him it now.

I fell while fishing,
went down the bank
and into the rocks.
Had to climb out,
hike up a long, switch-
back trail home.
Days later, I fished again
that spot
where I had fallen.

Two Canada geese honk their way
across the Gibbon River.
O to be so coupled and bold.

My, the flies are small
this early in the season.
So too the fish.

O to be in Nature,
where every chance
meeting between creatures
is an event.

*Dedicated to Neysa and Alicia, who made this reflection—and many others—possible.*

Kevin Rabas

## [the sign of the rabbit]

I have wanted
peace, a current
of lukewarm
water from the tap
on blood-red, winter-chilled
hands, a trout stream
at 62 degrees
when you are covered from
the waist down
in plastic waders,
when you are covered now
in your own salt water,
& relief can only come now
from the stream.
That is how I love you.
w/ the peace of satiation,
w/ relief, & w/ desire
for no more.

**[tea cups]**

We bought each other
tea cups one afternoon.
We'll keep them
at your place, we agree.

Our coins collect on top the dresser.
Our clothes mix on the floor.

We press against each other
in the doorway, winter
around us, like steam
above a cup.

Kevin Rabas

**[note for Lisa]**

My love, after reciting
poems onto the tail end
of your three-song demo tape,
I am reminded of how smart
your lyrics are, how finely
crafted, and how true.

How lucky I am
to share a place with you,
to hear your words and voice
nights, and hear your heart
as it shifts, as it speeds,
like the gazelle's.

Love,
Kevin

*Shawnee Mission Park, 14 September 1999, 10:40 am*

## [painting the walls together]

I use the roller,
and you edge in between
with the brush.
Our walls will be
white tonight.

The orange smoke stains
gone. Tonight, this is my place,
but tomorrow it will be ours.

Already you know the sound
of my shoes on the steps
to your door. Soon you will
know the sound of my bare feet
on our hardwood floor.

## [painting the walls together #2]

Washing the paint roller in the sink,
wringing the paint and water from the muff,
I remember how I once reached for you
as I would for a ripe bunch of fruit,
and I think of Chekov's Gurov
who, with his knife,
slices into a ripe watermelon
instead of tending to his new lover—
you know the moment—
he ignores her little lap dog, nuzzled at his feet.
Sometimes all we really need
is enough fresh fruit.

**Always, my love, you fill me**
with wonder, make my body glow
like a pack of candles
posted, that burn
until the top of the cake
is pooled
with wax.

## Isabelle

Isabelle, a wire
    dress model,
leans against a brick wall
    you've painted white.
She's not your size, but you keep her,
    a sister w/o wants—
only clothing, pinned fabric.
Already I love her enough
to see through her wires & not see brick,
not see ribbon, needles, thread, but see
you, see what you keep
    when throughout your many moves
you've left behind so much.

## The Neighbors

I am learning their habits:
when they flush, when they enter
and exit, whether they slam or pull
the door shut, whether they yell
and beat one another deep in the night,
whether they make love at midnight
or at noon, and for how long, and who
cries out the loudest, who goes for milk
early in the morning, who starts
the car, scrapes ice, who cooks
and for how long, and using which pans,
that clang, and how often
they set off the smoke alarm.

**[waiting for you]**

& the book is open
on its stand,
the mirror shined & newly hung
    across from the bed.

All the dresser drawers
    are full
      & closed,

& I am waiting
    for you
    to help me

remove,
    tangle
        irreparably,
all our sheets.

# Plays

# Lemonade
(a ten-minute play)

Kevin Rabas

Characters:
JAMES: M, late 20s to mid 30s
ISABELLE: F, approximately 10 years older than JAMES, late 30s to mid 40s, hairstylist

Time & Place:
Present day, salon, JAMES in styling chair

### Original Production

*Lemonade* was first fully performed in 2014 at the Warehouse Performing Arts Center in Charlotte, North Carolina.

JAMES | Daniel Breuer
ISABELLE | Meredith McBride

JAMES: Don't I know you? Wait. It'll come to me. (*Beat*) No.

ISABELLE: Where're you from, sweetie?

JAMES: Here. I grew up in Shawnee.

ISABELLE: What street?

JAMES: 59th and Haskins.

ISABELLE: Really? I dated a guy over there. People called him "Smooth." His name was Harold.

JAMES: I knew "Smooth." He lived across the street. Always had a group of cool kids around him and his big black Camaro.

ISABELLE: Cool kids? I'll bet I was one of them. Did you hang with him?

JAMES: No, I was 10 then. Too young. And shy. I sold those high schoolers lemonade.

ISABELLE: Really?

JAMES: And, one day, this beautiful red-haired girl, instead of giving me a tip, gave me a kiss on the cheek I never forgot. Chalked it up as one of the finest days of my youth. A kiss as a tip.

ISABELLE: Really?

JAMES: Couldn't be you, though. You're blonde.

ISABELLE: Yes, I am, sweets. Through and through. (*She tugs at a strand of her hair, points to the roots.*) (*Beat*) Who usually cuts your hair?

JAMES: Supercuts.

ISABELLE: Really? Kind of cheap, huh, sugar?

JAMES: Just not picky, I guess.

ISABELLE: (*Coy*) Sure you can afford me?

JAMES: I'll do my best. (*Beat*) Maybe I just lack style. Can you give me style?

ISABELLE: Anything I do for you will give you more style than you already have.

JAMES: Really?

ISABELLE: Trust me. I know what I'm doing. This is my place. This is what I do. (*Beat*) Business cut?

JAMES: Sure, business cut.

ISABELLE: Feathered around the ears?

JAMES: Sure. (*Beat*) What's your name?

ISABELLE: Isabelle.

JAMES: James. Good to meet you. Style me up, will ya? Like Buddy Bolden might.

ISABELLE: Who?

JAMES: Buddy Bolden, the first jazz musician. He was a barber days; played his flugelhorn nights. Walked in front at the Mardi

Gras parade, bright horn to the clouds, a new song coming from that magic flugelhorn. The first brilliant soloist.

**ISABELLE**: Really? I don't play.

**JAMES**: Sing?

**ISABELLE**: Only in the shower.

**JAMES**: Do you like jazz?

**ISABELLE**: You mean like Kenny G?

**JAMES**: More like Charlie Parker, Miles, Coltrane, Keith Jarrett.

**ISABELLE**: They any good?

**JAMES**: Let me tell ya, they make Kenny G look like Fabio just *holding* a horn.

**ISABELLE**: Is that bad?

**JAMES**: Well, at least G *looks* good.

**ISABELLE**: You sure you want a business cut? Maybe you need something jazzier.

**JAMES**: Any hair left?

**ISABELLE**: Enough. Want it a little longer in the back?

**JAMES**: Your call. Make me stylin'.

**ISABELLE**: I'll make your hair hot. Hot as I can. Ready for that?

**JAMES**: I could use some heat. Some Armstrong's Hot Five heat.

**ISABELLE**: Cute girls will turn their heads to look at you, when I'm through.

**JAMES**: I could use some of that.

**ISABELLE**: Really? You seem like you'd get plenty of looks, sweets.

**JAMES**: Maybe. (*Beat*) No. Not so much.

**ISABELLE**: I'll bet you're a charmer at work.

**JAMES**: I wouldn't notice. I teach college. Undergrads are off limits.

**ISABELLE**: Must be tough. What do you teach?

**JAMES**: English Composition days. And play jazz nights.

**ISABELLE**: Make a lot?

**JAMES**: No, but pay those bills. I guess that's why—

**ISABELLE & JAMES**: Supercuts!

**JAMES**: You're sweet.

**ISABELLE**: Sweet? I'm probably a decade older than you. Sure I'm not—

**JAMES**: I might be able to catch up.

**ISABELLE**: Can't outrun time.

JAMES: I can try. I listen to music decades before my time. Spin the LPs, try to bring that sound into my hands, sticks.

ISABELLE: Drummers. Time keepers. Rumblers.

JAMES: No, drummers are more than that. Drums are the drug, the poetry, the kiss.

ISABELLE: The kiss?

JAMES: What starts it all—a touch, a kiss.

ISABELLE: Not bad.

JAMES: That kiss with the lemonade. It jumpstarted my mouth.

ISABELLE: Really?

JAMES: It drummed in my blood for years. All I could think of was that girl—

ISABELLE: Who tipped with a kiss.

JAMES: I've seen and known wilder things since, but that was the hottest. Honest and sweet and simple.

ISABELLE: For a little guy.

JAMES: For a kid who only had lemonade, a cup full of lemonade.

ISABELLE: I'll bet that got you going, trigger.

JAMES: Still does.

ISABELLE: You know, I have a confession, James.

JAMES: What's that?

ISABELLE: My hair's not always been blonde.

JAMES: How?

ISABELLE: I dye it. I dyed it in high school.

JAMES: Really? (*Beat*) Red?

ISABELLE: Yep.

JAMES: So you were—

ISABELLE: Yep, sweets. I was that girl.

JAMES: My first kiss.

ISABELLE: Right on the cheek.

JAMES: But I heard that red-head was in a bad wreck. "Smooth" took a country road curve way too fast and flipped that car, messed up him and his girl. Plastic surgery to the face. You look too good to be her.

ISABELLE: (*Pulling her hair back*) Scars. Even now. I keep my hair long enough to cover them.

JAMES: I'm sorry. I'm so sorry.

ISABELLE: It's ok, kid.

JAMES: You're still a true beauty to me, Isabelle. Scars and all.

ISABELLE: You're just saying that.

(JAMES *touches her scars*.)

JAMES: No. I mean it. I love every bit of your terrain.

ISABELLE: Really? Every bit? (*Coy*) There's more to know.

JAMES: Bet there is. When do you get off work?

ISABELLE: You're my last one.

JAMES: Can I buy you a drink? I've got a place in mind.

ISABELLE: Far?

JAMES: Just 15 minutes.

ISABELLE: My part of town?

JAMES: Will broaden your horizons.

ISABELLE: Safe?

JAMES: Safe enough. Besides, you've got me.

ISABELLE: They serve vodka tonics?

JAMES: What, no lemonade? I thought you were a lemonade girl.

ISABELLE: That was a long time ago.

JAMES: You're gonna love it. This great place downtown at 18th and Vine. The Blue Room.

**ISABELLE**: You think I can like jazz?

**JAMES**: You'll love it. You'll savor this new music. Sweeter than any lemonade.

**ISABELLE**: Can anything be sweeter?

**JAMES**: Golden jazz can. Played by subterranean gods.

**ISABELLE**: Subterranean gods?

**JAMES**: You know, Kerouac, The Beats. Jazzers were their gods.

**ISABELLE**: Gods? Mine hangs on a cross.

**JAMES**: Then untack him. Take him down. And dance.

**ISABELLE**: Dance?

**JAMES**: Come with me. Let me turn our blood into wine.

**ISABELLE**: Fine. Bring on your jazz. Let's commune. (*Beat*) Know what?

**JAMES**: What?

**ISABELLE**: I like you, kid. Even more that you're grown.

**JAMES**: Really?

**ISABELLE**: Really. I'll travel with you, if only for a night.

(ISABELLE *pecks him on the cheek.*)

**JAMES**: I'll drive us for just as long as you want.

**ISABELLE**: And I'll try to keep my hands off you, while we go.

(*Long kiss*)

(*Lights fade*)

# Elves
(a ten-minute dark comedy)

Kevin Rabas

Characters:
CURTIS: M, 45, born and raised in a small town in central Kansas
JOY: F, 43, married to Curtis, born and raised in a small town in central Kansas

Time & Place:
Mid- to late-1990s, small house in a suburb of Kansas City

Props:
Table
Flower pot (with a flower inside)
Two chairs
Telephone (optional–characters may simply use a hand to mimic a telephone receiver using the hang-loose sign)

## Original Production

*Elves* was first performed in 1997 as a reader's theatre production in the Purple Masque Theatre at Kansas State University.

*Elves* saw a second reader's theatre production in 2009 at Emporia State University, directed by Kevin Rabas.

CURTIS | Robert Flaherty Hart
JOY | Antonia Felix

*Elves* was first fully performed in 2009 as part of the EMU Theatre's Locally Grown 10-Minute Play Festival in Lawrence, Kansas.

CURTIS | Philip Brown
JOY | Sharon Brown

(*Lights brighten on* CURTIS *and* JOY, *seated at a table. On the table is a flowerpot and a telephone.*)

JOY: You know something? I think you're still nuts about your mother.

CURTIS: Nuts?

JOY: Yeah. If she said hop, I'll bet you'd hop.

CURTIS: What do you mean?

JOY: I'll bet you're still *hers* after all these years. I'll bet if it came down between her and me, you'd choose her.

CURTIS: Where're you getting this?

JOY: An old woman called here this morning while you were sleeping. She must've been at least seventy and she sounded hysterical. She kept asking about her boy. I couldn't tell who they were. Must've been a wrong number. But for some reason I kept thinking the voice on the other end sounded suspiciously familiar. Almost like... Like your mother's...

CURTIS: Really? (*The phone rings.* CURTIS *picks up the receiver.*) Well, hello. Isn't this a surprise... Yeah, yeah, it's been rainin' here too, Ma... Oh about six inches over the past few days... Millie?... No, I didn't know she was out there. Did you two have a nice visit? ... Oh? ... Your elves? ... Now why would she want to do a thing like that? ... Ma, why would Millie even want your elves? ... Are you sure? ... Yeah, yeah I can fix up your locks and put a little peg hanger up for your keys. Right by the door... Sure. Sure, if another deadbolt's what you want, another deadbolt's what you'll get ... Now? I'll see what I can do. How about I come on out this weekend... Mighty fine... Me, too... Bye-bye.

JOY: So what'd she have to say?

CURTIS: Oh, everything seems to be fine. It's raining there, too. The milo's up, and the wheat's doing fine.

JOY: Fine? What was that about elves? Didn't she sound the slightest bit worked up?

CURTIS: No, she sounded fine. Only a few minor squabbles been goin' on lately.

JOY: Squabbles?

CURTIS: Oh, Millie'd been out to visit, and Ma accused her of stealing some of her stuff. Ma ended up calling her a bitch and throwing her out of the house, I guess. Guess they're not getting along. The usual.

JOY: But what was that about *elves*?

CURTIS: Oh, Ma accused Millie of stealing some... some little *elf ornaments* from off the tree along with some other of her stuff. Why she would want any of it I sure as hell don't know!

(*Beat*)

JOY: Is she still having troubles with Norman?

CURTIS: How should I know?

JOY: Didn't you just get through talking to her? (*Beat*) That's a shame, you know. Norman's such a nice man. Her age, too. He's probably the only available man in that whole town. He even brings her her groceries every week. Who else would bring them to her?

**CURTIS**: I don't know. Alvin, maybe.

**JOY**: Alvin? Sure. Sure he wouldn't. Oh, he'd start off by bringing them, but inevitably sooner or later he'd end up bringing her a whole dozen eggs instead of special requesting just two or three, and she'd blow up on him and start swatting him with that flyswatter again, and he'd give up on her. He'd just send that tramp of his, Thelma, over there about every two weeks or so with six tins of Spam, a bag of prunes, two jugs of grape juice, and a box of Metamucil. And that's all she'd get. She'd have to mooch or garden for the rest. (*beat*) Your mother should hang on to that Norman. Heck, she's run all her other friends off. She should hang on to that Norman. He's loyal. Any everybody knows that a man who's loyal is better than any dog.

**CURTIS**: What?

**JOY**: A man who's... never mind.

(*The phone rings.*)

**JOY**: (*Picking up the receiver*) What! One moment. One— Who *is* this? ... You're going to ... shoot who?

**CURTIS**: Who is it?

**JOY**: Ma'am are you sure you have the right household? Wait! Calm down, please. Are you sure you have the... Now listen, if you don't tell me exactly who this is, I'm going to have to hang up on you... No, if you don't tell me... No, please listen. If you don't tell me... I'm sorry. (*Hanging up*) Goodbye.

**CURTIS**: Who was that?

**JOY**: How should I know? Some loony, I guess.

(*The phone rings.*)

JOY: Take it off the hook! (*Or:* "*Turn it off.*")

CURTIS: What if it's important? What if... (*Picking up the receiver*) Hello. What... What! ... Slow down, Ma, you're talkin' a mile a minute.

JOY: Your mother! Again!

CURTIS: (CURTIS *nods.*) (*Plodding*) No, I don't think Norman's gonna smother you during the night with a Ziplok bag... No, Ma.

JOY: What's the matter with her?

CURTIS: No, Ma. Why do you think that? ... No *particular reason*! You had a *dream* about it! ... No, Ma. Ma, have you been reading the Bible before Oprah comes on again? ... No, Ma... Yes, Ma. I don't like Sally either... Raf-uh Raf-ee-Al... Yeah, Ma... Italian... No, I didn't know she had her own salad dressing. (*Beat*) Ma, what about Norman? ... Your neighbor Norman... Yes, that Norman, though I wouldn't call him *that*. Isn't he your friend? Doesn't he bring you your groceries? ... Just try and be a little nicer to him, Ma. And *put that gun away*! Unload it and give it back to Alvin... I mean it. Unload it and give it back to Alvin first thing tomorrow morning... Ok... I'm fine... She's fine... Good night. (*Hangs up*)

JOY: So it *was* your mother. How could I have known? She didn't say who she was.

CURTIS: You should know by now. You should know her voice.

JOY: Not when she's hysterical I shouldn't. You didn't either for a while there. I could tell. You couldn't tell who she was. She was raving. Why?

**CURTIS**: I guess Norman set her off. He brought back a dozen eggs again. And then there was something about those elves. I don't know. She'll be all right.

**JOY**: I've been thinking about those elf ornaments. How did your mother know Millie took them, anyway? Did she catch her stealing them?

**CURTIS**: No. She said she noticed them there before, just hanging on the tree, and then toward the end of Millie's visit—oh, the last day or so, when Millie was packing up—Ma discovered those elves of hers weren't hanging on the tree anymore.

**JOY**: So she accused Millie?

**CURTIS**: I guess.

**JOY**: Did she check her suitcase?

**CURTIS**: No, Millie wouldn't let her. And, on her way out, Ma said she noticed that Millie's suitcase was draggin'. And, on her way in, Ma said Millie'd had *no trouble* with it. So Ma ran out there and started yellin' at Millie, callin' her all sorts of names, accusing her of stealin' her elves. But who cares about elves! I'm more concerned about Ma handlin' a gun. She never learned how. She could hurt someone.

**JOY**: How could she *not* learn. You mean to tell me she lived on a farm her whole life and never once learned how to use a gun?

**CURTIS**: Yep. Never learned how to drive either.

**JOY**: I don't believe it! And I don't believe that those elves would've weighed down Millie's bag so much that it would've made it drag, either. Now would it've?

CURTIS: I guess not.

JOY: Would it've?

CURTIS: Hey, that's all she said. And all I can go on is what she said.

JOY: And why would Millie've even wanted those elves in the first place? They couldn't have been worth much.

CURTIS: Hey, that's all she said. She said she thinks Millie stole the elves.

JOY: And what do you think?

CURTIS: I don't know. All I've got to go on is what Ma said.

JOY: You know your mother has not always been the most rational person in the world. You know she's a little bit loony sometimes. Has she been taking her medication?

CURTIS: I don't know. I didn't ask.

JOY: You should know. We should call her doctor and see what she's on. Maybe it's not agreeing with her. The nerve of her! Calling us, not telling us who she is, threatening to shoot Norman!

CURTIS: She said she was afraid.

JOY: Afraid of what? Norman's harmless. Where did she get the idea he'd come after her anyway? They're relation, aren't they? Second cousins or something? Aren't they all related in that whole town of Russell?

**CURTIS**: Yeah, damn near related, at least. Sure, the whole lot of 'em are. What's your point?

**JOY**: So, she shouldn't have anything to worry about with Norman. They're kin.

**CURTIS**: That wouldn't stop any of them. Remember, Ma thinks Millie stole her elves.

**JOY**: Come on. You know she's probably just making that up to get back at Millie. That's what those sisters are like, it has nothing to do with kin… well, normal kin. It's just *your* family that's that way. My family's never been that way. It's *your* family that's tragic. Anyway, hasn't this happened before? Haven't your mother and Millie accused each other of all sorts of things, like robbing each other's inheritance every time someone dies? Don't you remember when Aunt Bea passed last Christmas, and all she left behind was a chest full of slag jewelry: those monstrous globs of pewter and brass with chips of colored glass glued to their fronts. Who'd want those anyway? But those sisters picked it over in a rage, like two hungry chickens pecking beak to beak over only *half* a worm. Last time we visited, didn't I spot your mother wearing a pair of Aunt Bea's earrings?

**CURTIS**: I don't know. But Ma's sure Millie took her elves.

**JOY**: How can she be? She didn't even see her take 'em. And why do you have to be the one to go out there and settle her down? You're always the one who goes out and does that. Alvin's closer. Why not let him do it? Don't you remember? We made plans for this weekend.

**CURTIS**: I know, I know. I'm sorry honey, but—

JOY: What about the walk in the park? We're going to see the eagles! The eagles that nest in the highest branches of the sycamores surrounding the landfill. We're going to walk down those grey paths of dust hand in hand, paths of dust like the dust on the moon. Sacred. Timeless. Untouched. Don't you remember?

CURTIS: Sure, I remember, but I've got to go. We can go next weekend, I promise.

JOY: Sure!

CURTIS: Really—Ma's upset.

JOY: Loony, I'd say. Don't you remember the story the Holcombs always tell about your mother, about when you three boys were just toddling around?

CURTIS: Don't remind me.

JOY: About when right after she had Alvin, her third child, she said God told her to go up top the roof and drop her own boys off. She must've been reading the Good Book a little too closely right around then. Remember that part about Abraham dragging his only son up on top the mountain to sacrifice him to the Lord? Remember?

CURTIS: I don't know.

JOY: I do. The Holcombs tell it every Christmas, and about how they just happened to be driving by that morning, and just happened to catch Ma up there, with the three of you in her arms, getting ready to chuck you on off the roof.

CURTIS: Ma had a hard time right after Alvin. Chalk it up to post-what-da-ya-call-it depression.

JOY: Portum.

CURTIS: What?

JOY: Post Portum Depression.

CURTIS: Portum? I thought it was Partum.

JOY: Whatever.

CURTIS: Well, whatever they call it, she had a hard go of it. Alvin's was not an easy birth. So can't you be a little more sympathetic? Can't you understand? So she—

JOY: So she's always been a little dramatic. She's always been a little on the loony side. Millie didn't steal those elves. Norman's harmless. Alvin will take care of it. There's no reason for you to go out there.

CURTIS: I'm going.

JOY: You believe her, don't you? You believe her about those elves! You're just as loony as she is!

CURTIS: She said she thinks Millie stole 'em.

JOY: Let me tell you something. If I ever go loony, and I'm just wandering around the house, accusing people of stealing all my stuff, accusing people of plotting to murder me when they're my only friends in the whole damn town, and in general, in danger of hurting myself, and I refuse to go to the doctor's, no matter how hard you try to persuade me or trick me to get there, I would want you to bonk me over the head and drag me there. *Get me some help*, would you! Wouldn't you want the same?

**CURTIS**: I don't know. I guess. I'm going to pack.

**JOY**: No. Would you or wouldn't you?

**CURTIS**: I'd have to think about it.

**JOY**: Would you bonk me over the head and drag me to help or not!

**CURTIS**: I'd try to help you.

**JOY**: But *would* you?

**CURTIS**: I just don't think I could bonk you over the head.

**JOY**: What's stopping you?

**CURTIS**: My conscience.

**JOY**: Forget that! Think of me falling further and further into my own insanity. You could catch me. You could catch me in time. You could save me. You could—

**CURTIS**: But by dragging you off? Against your will? You'd hate me for it!

**JOY**: I'd love you for it. I'd understand.

**CURTIS**: I doubt it. Never!

**JOY**: Look. Look, you lousy, good-for-nothin', weak, moma's man, still taking orders from your former matriarch! You'd better listen up! If I ever go crazy, I expect you to bonk me over the head and drag me off! Got it!

**CURTIS**: Wait!

**JOY**: (*Interrupting*) I'd do the same for you! I'd drag you off to help! I'd drag you off as soon as I knew!

**CURTIS**: But how would you know?

**JOY**: I'd know. I'd bash your skull in with a flower pot! I'd take you by the belt-loop and drag you down the stairs and into the Bronco. I'd be gentle! I'd be gentle with you after putting up with all of your madness for so long! I'd be gentle! You could trust me on that! You'd be as fresh and unharmed as a newborn child when I took you in to sign the register at the loony bin. I'd cradle you. I'd pet you. I'd—(*CURTIS bonks JOY over the head.*)

(*Pause*)

Come on, you can do better than that!

(*JOY reaches for the flowerpot.*) (*Both CURTIS and JOY are poised ready to strike.*) (*The lights dim.*)

(*Curtain*)

# The Broken Cup
(a ten-minute play)

*First Couple*
Characters:
JESSE: M, 21
BEA: F, 22

Time & Place:
Present day, a midwestern college, in Bea's apartment kitchen

Props:
Coffee cup

*Second Couple*
Characters:
MAN: M, 25
WOMAN: F, 23, very pregnant

Time & Place:
Present day, one year following the first scene, same place as above

Props:
Small kitchen wastebasket
Pillow
Coffee cup (identical to the one above, but with Sharpie black lines, representing cracks in the cup)

**Original Production**

*The Broken Cup* was first fully performed in 2013 at the Ad Astra Theatre Ensemble 24-Hour Play Festival in Topeka, Kansas.

JESSE | Ben Deghand
BEA | Kristin Ross
MAN | Devin Deman
WOMAN | Carmelle Hayes

(*Lights up*)

BEA: We'll break this coffee cup, when we break up, and we'll be done. The first thing we got together will be the first thing to go.

JESSE: It's beautiful. You keep it. We don't need to smash it now, and, who knows, we might not split.

BEA: You mean marry?

JESSE: You never know.

(BEA *kisses* JESSE.)

BEA: Babe, I know. You're sweet. Sweet, sweet, Jesse. I love you. If not with you, I'll break this alone. There's only one way this one will end, and it's with a broken cup.

JESSE: But, Bea, the cup stands for more than us. It's art. Fine art. Just look at it, with those glazed and fired lines of colored paint, with that mature patina.

BEA: Patina? Big word.

JESSE: Patina. Sense of age, maturity. Like rust on metal, time's hand in the paint.

BEA: Not bad.

JESSE: And some potter spent a week or even a month on this line of cups, and ours is just one of a set. Pryde's in Westport was lucky this time. They got some good cups, cups that are art.

BEA: It's beautiful, but it also stands for us. So, when we're through, it goes.

**JESSE**: Would you kill a little bird that sang for us or kill a kitten we'd bought together?

**BEA**: No. But I'd give it away. Neither of us could have it. It'd be too full of us.

**JESSE**: Let's just plan to stay together and keep the cup.

**BEA**: Everything ends. We're in college. When we're done, you'll go one way, and I'll go another. That's how school works.

**JESSE**: But, what if I don't mind? What if I follow you?

**BEA**: Then, there'll be nothing for you but misery. I'll dump you, and you'll be alone in a town you don't know, with no job, and very little love.

**JESSE**: You wouldn't break us, like a cup.

**BEA**: I would. I will. Just you watch.

**JESSE**: Give me that cup. I don't trust you with it. I'll keep it for us.

**BEA**: You won't break it, though. And I won't let you keep it.

**JESSE**: I can break it just as well as you. I can break it right now, call it quits. I can let you go. I can let us go.

**BEA**: No, you can't. You never could.

**JESSE**: (*Taking the cup and raising it above his head*) Now I have it. I have what stands for us.

**BEA**: (*Kicking him in the shins so that* JESSE *doubles over, and* BEA *takes the cup.*) You can't be trusted with it. You're too weak, too sentimental.

(BEA *drops the cup and breaks it.*)

**JESSE**: So it's over?

**BEA**: Just look at the cup.

**JESSE**: I'll get us a new one. I'll get us two.

**BEA**: Just promise to smash yours, if that's how we end up.

**JESSE**: I'll get us a whole set of cups.

**BEA**: Children?

**JESSE**: Let's just see how far we go.

**BEA**: We'll let *them* break our cups. Kids are good at breaking. Just you watch. They'll break us.

**JESSE**: I think I'll buy carpet then, put it in the kitchen even, all throughout the house, so nothing will break, nothing will smash, even when dropped from on top of the couch or even the countertop.

**BEA**: Kids can find ways. They can jump and stomp. Our cups won't last. And we won't either.

**JESSE**: I'll buy only plastic cups.

**BEA**: (*Beat, considering*) We might last. We might last on plastic cups.

(JESSE *picks up pieces of the broken cup. Tip: select large, non-sharp pieces.*)

**JESSE**: I'll glue it back together.

**BEA**: I'll break it again.

**JESSE**: I'll use super glue. I'll keep it up high. You won't see it, won't know it's there.

**BEA**: If I find it, I'll break it.

**JESSE**: I'll find another one. I'll replace it with a plastic cup.

**BEA**: That can't be fine art, a plastic cup. Fine art doesn't come in plastic, the material of children and the sick.

**JESSE**: Art lasts, though, like plastic. Plastic is eternal. Well, mostly so. Only extreme heat or cold can nix it. Not a drop. Not a kick or a smash or a chop. Plastic lasts, like us. Plastic lasts.

**BEA**: Let's hope so. For your sake, let's hope.

(JESSE *holds pieces of the cup out in his cupped hands, and* BEA *clasps her hands around his.*)

(*Blackout*)

(*Same scene, one year later. Lights up*)

**MAN**: I found this cup. It seems to be glued back together.

**WOMAN**: Where?

**MAN**: On the counter.

WOMAN: Strange thing to leave.

MAN: (*Taking cup and motioning toward the trash can*) Out with the old; in with the new.

WOMAN: Wait.

MAN: What?

WOMAN: Let's keep it.

MAN: Why?

WOMAN: Like a memento. An emblem of people past. A keepsake. A ghost's bones.

MAN: Ghost's bones?

WOMAN: Relic of the former owners of this old apartment. Like a skeleton of their lives.

MAN: (*Puzzled, questioning*) Ok…

WOMAN: Ok! We'll keep it. But where should we keep it?

MAN: In the cupboard?

WOMAN: No. It's a relic.

MAN: (*Lightly mocking*) Ghost's bones?

WOMAN: How about in the baby's room? The old and the new. (*Rubbing her baby bump*)

**MAN**: That way, if it gets knocked off by the baby, oh well, it's already broken.

**WOMAN**: Seriously? Show some respect for the departed.

**MAN**: We don't even know them.

**WOMAN**: Let's imagine them. How about he's a wealthy businessman, often away. He brings home this mug, but it cracked in his bag on the plane, broken at 20 thousand feet.

**MAN**: And his wife says, "Hey, some gift! It's broken."

**WOMAN**: No. She's touched. She glues it back together with love, and they trade sips from it. A lover's breakfast, lover's feast.

**MAN**: With a broken cup. They get cut. Her lip bleeds.

WOMAN: And he licks it clean.

**MAN**: (*Laughs, mocking*) Ultra-romantic.

**WOMAN**: True romance. Blood and cuts and all. (*Beat*) Or... It's the first time a toddler drinks from a real cup, not a *plastic* cup.

**MAN**: And everything goes fine until—

**WOMAN**: Having drank the whole cup down without a mishap, the toddler shakes her hands in glee—

**MAN**: Knocking the cup over and onto the tile floor.

**WOMAN**: But Moma wants the memento, so she glues it back together for her "big girl."

**MAN**: (*Leading, mocking*) Touching.

**WOMAN**: Real life, broken cups and all.

**MAN**: Ok. We keep it.

**WOMAN**: Ghost's bones. (*Beat*) Something for our big girl to drink from one day.

(*Pantomime: He fills the cup with liquid, offers her a drink. WOMAN drinks, then offers MAN a sip. MAN sips. MAN & WOMAN kiss.*)

(*Blackout*)

# Baby on a Plane
(a ten-minute play)

Characters:
JAMES: M, early 40s
ISABELLE ("Izzy"): F, early 50s, married to James
TIFFANY: F, 20s-30s, attractive, single, self-focused
FLIGHT ATTENDANT: F, 40s-50s

Time & Place: Present day, airplane cabin

Props:
TIFFANY
Large doll (as baby)
Stuffed animal toys (2-3)
Black and white photo
Bag of Fruit Loops
Backpack
Bag or purse
ISABELLE
Purse
Bag of mini-carrots
FLIGHT ATTENDANT
Peppermints
ALSO
Folding chairs (4 or more)
Carry-on bags (for any) (optional)

## Original Production

*Baby on a Plane* was first fully performed in 2016 at the Ad Astra Theatre Ensemble's 24-Hour Play Festival in Topeka, Kansas. The production was directed by Erin McGinnis.

JAMES | Scott Kickhaefer
ISABELLE | Annie Wilcox
TIFFANY | Marjorie Lathrop
FLIGHT ATTENDANT | Michelle Carson

(*Enter JAMES and ISABELLE. A series of chairs demarcate an improvised airline seating area, including an aisle for the FLIGHT ATTENDANT.*)

**ISABELLE**: What's your seat number?

**JAMES**: 2B

**ISABELLE**: I'm 3A. They've got us separated.

**JAMES**: It'll be ok.

**ISABELLE**: Frickin' airlines.

**JAMES**: Really. It'll be ok. (*To invisible passenger*) Excuse me.

(*He sits.*)

**ISABELLE:** Of all the things! Should've flown Southwest.

(*ISABELLE sits in a row in front of JAMES.*)
(*Enter TIFFANY, with baby. She puts her butt in JAMES's face to situate her bag.*)

**TIFFANY**: Excuse me.

(*JAMES tries to keep his cool.*)

**JAMES**: (*To the baby*) Hi there, little one.

(*Enter FLIGHT ATTENDANT, checking the overhead compartments and slamming the compartments shut, while marching down the aisle.*)

**FLIGHT ATTENDANT**: (*To TIFFANY*) She's a beauty.

**TIFFANY**: Keeps me busy.

**FLIGHT ATTENDANT**: Good sign. (*To the baby*) How are you, little miss? (*To* TIFFANY) She's a cute chunk. That's good.

**TIFFANY**: Why?

**FLIGHT ATTENDANT**: That means more food to her brain. She'll be smart.

**TIFFANY**: Smart? That's a change.

**FLIGHT ATTENDANT**: It's good for girls to be smart. Brilliant even.

**TIFFANY**: And pretty. Only if she's pretty.

**FLIGHT ATTENDANT**: Double threat. Brains and beauty. She'll lead a charmed life. Lucky mother.

**TIFFANY**: Lucky girl.
**FLIGHT ATTENDANT**: Lucky little one.

**TIFFANY**: You are cute and smart. (*Kisses the baby*) Kiss, kiss. (*Kisses the baby*)

**FLIGHT ATTENDANT**: And will be.

(*Exit* FLIGHT ATTENDANT)

(TIFFANY *plays with a toy with the baby, holding the toy towards the baby, then pulling the toy away. The toy gets tossed into the aisle near* JAMES. JAMES *and* TIFFANY *both look at the toy.* TIFFANY *doesn't go for the toy, so* JAMES *does. He hands the toy to* TIFFANY. ISABELLE *notices and scoffs.*)

**TIFFANY**: Thanks! So chivalrous.

**JAMES**: I try. She's cute. And smart. Our flight attendant was right.

**TIFFANY**: Hope so. The world could use more brains. (*Putting a Fruit Loop into the baby's mouth*) That's what I think, and I try to feed her smart stuff.

**JAMES**: Fruit Loops aren't half bad.

**TIFFANY**: Not too much in them.

**JAMES**: True.

**TIFFANY**: And fruit. Lots of fruit. But you can't bring real fruit on a flight.

**JAMES**: Who's gonna bomb a plane with a banana?

**TIFFANY**: No one. See what I mean?

(TIFFANY *kisses the baby, plays with the baby's feet, kisses the baby's toes.*)

**ISABELLE**: (*Whispers to* JAMES) Fruit Loops really aren't any good for you. Look at how many things are on the list. Ingredients gone wild!

**JAMES**: (*Whispers back*) They're not that bad.

**ISABELLE**: They're not that good.

(TIFFANY *stoops to get into a bag at her feet and slips and falls into* JAMES's *lap. He tries to play it cool, cavalier, gentlemanly.* TIFFANY *turns to the baby in her airplane seat and puts her butt in* JAMES's *face.* ISABELLE *reacts.*)

**JAMES**: (*Awkwardly*) Close quarters.

**TIFFANY**: I don't mind. I like being social.

(ISABELLE *raises an eyebrow.*)

**JAMES**: How old is she?

**TIFFANY**: One.

**JAMES**: What's her name?

**TIFFANY**: Millicent. Millie, for short. And I hope, like her name, she comes into riches.

**JAMES**: Millions of cents?

**ISABELLE**: That doesn't even make sense.
**TIFFANY**: What do you do?

**JAMES**: Teach composition at Cowley Community College.

**TIFFANY**: Notes? Music?

**JAMES**: No, freshman English papers.

**TIFFANY**: Sounds glamorous. Does it pay well?

**JAMES**: Not enough.

TIFFANY: Enough to make this flight?

JAMES: Just enough.

TIFFANY: You look trustworthy. (*Introducing herself*) Tiffany.

JAMES: James.

TIFFANY: James, would you watch little Millie? I need to pee.

(TIFFANY *hands the baby along with some stuffed animal toys—Babar elephants, Mickey Mouse—to* JAMES, *who is a little shocked at this gesture. Exit* TIFFANY)

ISABELLE: The nerve.

JAMES: It's just a kid.

ISABELLE: Like a hot potato, tossed around. And all of that crap food, and that damn throw toy. She's a piece of work.

JAMES: Everybody struggles. (*Re: the baby*) You want one?

ISABELLE: Not that one.

JAMES: She seems cute.

ISABELLE: Full of sugar.

JAMES: Don't folks say "sugar" and mean sweet, mean nice?

ISABELLE: Some folks do.

JAMES: So what they should say is rice or potatoes?

ISABELLE: That would help. That would be a start. Starch.

JAMES: How long's it been?

ISABELLE: Been what?

JAMES: Since we talked about having a child, Izzy?

ISABELLE: Talked about or done something about it?

JAMES: Either.

ISABELLE: Not long enough.

JAMES: Oh, come on. You mean you don't want one? (*Holding the child up, then playing with the baby and the toys*)

ISABELLE: Too much for me. Too much for us. We have work, things to accomplish.

JAMES: Couldn't we accomplish both?

ISABELLE: You could. Men always say that. And women do all the work.

JAMES: (*Re: the baby*) But she sure is cute. (*Playing with the baby and the toys*)

ISABELLE: Both of them are. Mother, daughter. Too cute!

JAMES: Can't be too cute.

ISABELLE: Yes, you can. What's Daisy in *Gatsby* say? Be a "beautiful little fool."

JAMES: You're beautiful, and you're no fool.

ISABELLE: Let's keep it that way, ok?

(*Enter* FLIGHT ATTENDANT)

FLIGHT ATTENDANT: (*To* ISABELLE) Peppermint?

ISABELLE: No.

FLIGHT ATTENDANT: (*To* JAMES) Peppermint?

JAMES: No thanks.

FLIGHT ATTENDANT: So, now you've got the baby?

ISABELLE: Not for long.

FLIGHT ATTENDANT: But, man, is she cute. And smart. Walks right up into your heart.

ISABELLE: And later breaks it.
(*Exit* FLIGHT ATTENDANT)

(*Enter* TIFFANY)

TIFFANY: (*To* JAMES) Thanks. You're a peach.

(TIFFANY *takes the baby and the toys.*)

JAMES: No problem.

TIFFANY: You did great. You should have one.

**ISABELLE**: No.

**JAMES**: Maybe one day.

**TIFFANY**: (*To* ISABELLE) Don't wait too long.

**ISABELLE**: Don't hold your breath.

**TIFFANY**: (*To the baby*) Mommy missed you. (*Kisses the baby*) Kiss, kiss. (*Kisses the baby*)

**ISABELLE**: Where are you two going?

**TIFFANY**: The beach. To see my sister and her little poochies. See? (*She holds the photo to* ISABELLE *and then the baby, pointing*) There's your cousin Dora, and there's her little sister, Darlene.

**ISABELLE**: Precious. You look like you know the beach well.

**TIFFANY**: Thanks. It's good for the heart, good for the skin.

**ISABELLE**: Oh really? Meeting a man there?

**TIFFANY**: We'll see.

**ISABELLE**: You know, you don't need one. A man.

**TIFFANY**: But I might like one.

**ISABELLE**: (*Placing a hand on* JAMES) I'm glad I've got mine.

**TIFFANY**: He's so good with kids.

**ISABELLE**: A lost calling.

**TIFFANY**: Too, too bad.

(*The baby chucks a toy into the aisle.* JAMES *picks the toy up and hands the toy to* TIFFANY.)

Thanks again.

**JAMES**: Not a problem.

**ISABELLE**: (*To* JAMES) Might be.

(*Enter* FLIGHT ATTENDANT)

**FLIGHT ATTENDANT**: (*To* TIFFANY *and the baby*) We're making our final descent. Buckle up.

**TIFFANY**: Ok. Thank you.

**FLIGHT ATTENDANT**: Not a problem. You get that girl into a good school. And buy her lots and lots of books.

**TIFFANY**: Maybe she'll be a career girl, like her. (*Re:* ISABELLE)

**FLIGHT ATTENDANT**: That's not a bad way. She could also fly. Like me.

**TIFFANY**: I'd like that. Before we're locked in, could you help me with my bag?

**FLIGHT ATTENDANT**: Sure.

(*The* FLIGHT ATTENDANT *does, helping* TIFFANY *with a baby backpack from the overhead compartment.*)

**TIFFANY**: Thanks.

**FLIGHT ATTENDANT**: Sure thing.

(*Exit* FLIGHT ATTENDANT. *The plane lands; the passengers lurch forward.*)

(*The pack now on,* TIFFANY *fumbles to keep the pack upright and zipped. Everyone watches, waits. At last,* JAMES *helps her, zipping and adjusting the pack.*)

**TIFFANY**: Thanks. 'bout as bad as a bra strap.

**JAMES**: I'll bet.

(TIFFANY *looks at* JAMES *a little suggestively. She touches his cheek.*)

(TIFFANY *exits.* JAMES *watches her go.*)

**ISABELLE**: Don't even think about it.

**JAMES**: What?

**ISABELLE**: We don't need a child.

**JAMES**: Oh.

**ISABELLE**: You hungry? I've got plenty of snacks in my purse. (*Digs in purse and pulls out a bag of carrots*)

(JAMES *looks out, reflects.*)

(*Blackout*)

# Community Blood Bank
(a ten-minute play)

Kevin Rabas

Characters:
JANE: F, 22
CALVIN: M, 21

Time & Place:
1995, a bare stage with semblances of a community blood bank in Kansas City

Props:
Apparatus and blood bag (fills during the course of the play)
Other blood bank accoutrements, as desired
    OR
A portable white board
Easel
Red marker (a blood bag can be drawn on the white board, and JANE can draw more red on the board, to represent blood filling, as the play progresses)

### Original Production

*Community Blood Bank* was first presented in 2011 as a reader's theatre production at the Emporia State University Short Plays Festival. The production was directed by Lindsay Ward.

JANE | Kari Bowles
CALVIN | Tommy Govert

(*Lights up*)

**JANE**: I'll let you talk to me, while the bag fills. When the bag is full, you've got to leave.

(CALVIN *is newly hooked up to a blood bag—with just a small pool of blood at the bottom of the bag. As the play moves forward, the bag fills slowly with blood, and is completely filled at the end of the play.*)

**CALVIN**: Deal.

**JANE**: How'd you find me?

**CALVIN**: I asked Kathleen. I knew she'd know where you'd be. You look wonderful. Do you know that?

**JANE**: Thanks. I can walk again. Men like a girl that can walk on her own two legs. Sometimes they like the legs more than the girl. But you can't separate the legs from the girl. Well, usually you can't.

**CALVIN**: You had it bad last year, I know. That wheelchair didn't show off your legs much. But I still felt like a king dancing with you at the prom.

**JANE**: You were sweet to take me. My senior year.

**CALVIN**: Wheeling you around, holding your hand, then holding your gray rubber wheel. It was like dancing with a queen on her throne. And if I tired, I could sit in your lap.

**JANE**: You sure didn't. You're an old fool. In a young man's body.

**CALVIN**: Anyone would be a fool for you, Jane. Anyone.

**JANE**: So why'd you come, Calvin? You want to ask me out?

**CALVIN**: I thought you might have a doctor by now, but I thought I'd try.

**JANE**: I do. Too late. He's tall and handsome. 30. A newbee. Dr. Ryan Patrick Manfredson.

**CALVIN**: How can I compete?

**JANE**: Tell me stories. If you tell a good enough one, I may let you stay.

**CALVIN**: This sounds like the Arabian Nights, where a guy has to tell a gal stories, and keep talking, keep her listening. If he stops, he dies.

**JANE**: You don't have to raise the stakes that high. But keep talking. Tell me a story.

**CALVIN**: Ok. Here's a short one. My grandmother, from the sticks, always says she hates shrimp. But, she says, she loves those little horse-shoe shaped fish. Now what do you call them?

**JANE**: Shrimp. Not bad. Tell something longer.

**CALVIN**: In Munich, I told the ticket lady, "Send me to Barcelona," thinking of the beaches. It was raining all over Germany, a cold cobblestone rain. When I got on the train, it seemed to be taking too long, a day or two too long. In Rome, they said there were strikes with the trains, holding things up. I was supposed to go to Rome, then cross over into Spain. I asked the ticket puncher on the train, "Where are we going?" and he said, "Barcelona." The train drove onto a boat, and we landed. I got off and tried to change my money from dollars to pesos, but there was no one at the window. It was late, and dark. I asked a young cab driver to drive me to San Madra Familia, a place I was supposed to meet some friends and stay the night. He said, "Never heard of it," in a language I did not know. He asked another cab driver. No dice either. Eventually, they asked an old, old cab driver, and he too had never heard of it, and they led me into the station and to the station master, who said in Spanish, "Where are you going?" And I said, "Barcelona," and he said, "Espana or Sicilia?" And I said "Espana." He pointed to the floor, and drew a boot and island with his hand. "Sicilia," he said. "You're in Sicilia." He said, "Where will you sleep?" And it was my turn to point to the floor. "No," he said, and sent me in a cab to a Catholic wayside station. After that long night, I stayed with the station master a few days, until the train came back, and I could ride out of Sicily. Barcelona, Sicily. A little town in northeast Italy, where no one does Spanish dances, and the beaches are not always glorious, bright, and full.

JANE: Beautiful. You've turned into an adventurer since we were just kids in high school, haven't you? I've always wanted to travel, travel the world.

CALVIN: It's only been two years.

JANE: But a lot can happen in two years. To you.

CALVIN: To you, too. Look at you. You're helping people, saving people.

JANE: Just with blood.

CALVIN: (*He looks at his blood bag and turns a little queasy.*) Sure, with what else? With blood. (*Queasy*) With lots and lots of blood.

JANE: You're not going on me, are ya? You're not going to—

**CALVIN**: I hope not. But I feel it. I feel it going out of me now.

**JANE**: Hold on. How about you look right at me? Look right into my eyes as you talk.

**CALVIN**: That might help.

**JANE**: Try it.

**CALVIN**: I might enjoy it.

**JANE**: Try it. But don't get coy.

**CALVIN**: Ok. I was in New York with my sister, at the MOMA, Museum of Modern Art. There were crowds everywhere, so everyone had to stand. Every metal bench was packed. So, I was standing in front of this sculpture of a man rising out of the water. Neptune or something, and I just decided to stand there, and watch, and just look at that one statue for about half an hour. A cute young woman came by, and she looked at me with the curiosity that I was using on that statue, and I said to her, "If I stand here any longer, I'm going to become an exhibit." And she laughed. She gave me her number, and her first name. I wasn't looking to pick her up, but I said I was with my friends, and I might call her. We might all go somewhere together. About a month later, my sister calls me, and says she heard from the girl. There was an article in *The University Daily Kansan*. It was about pick-up lines that work. Mine was there. And there was her full name. Emily Hall.

**JANE**: The Lawrence sculptor?

**CALVIN**: Yes. I could've gone out with an artist, a rising star.

**JANE**: Why didn't you?

CALVIN: I didn't think of it. I was only looking at art.

JANE: Do you always think about art?

CALVIN: No. (*Musing*) Sometimes I think about people I love. Sometimes I think about you.

JANE: Honey, I'm taken. But remember, look at me when you talk. Look at me, always, when you talk.

CALVIN: Ok. Your eyes. I'll only look into your eyes.

JANE: Know any kids stories. I love little kids. We don't get many kids here, unless they've come with their parents. Tell me a kid story, can you?

CALVIN: My nephew's birthday was last week, and I sent him one of those "talking books," where you open each page and talk into this tiny spot where there are six little microphone holes, and when the kid opens the book out comes your voice—from across time, from across miles. Well, I mailed him the talking book, and I guess it got goofed up in the mail. My sister said when she opened it and flipped the pages, my voice was slow and distorted, otherworldly. She said Ethan calls it "scary book."

JANE: So you've done your part for young readers? You've made them run from *scary* books?

CALVIN: I've done all sorts of things for literacy.

JANE: You *are* an English major.

CALVIN: Yep, that's how it goes. A couple more years and I may be teaching *scary* books.

**JANE**: How's UMKC?

**CALVIN**: It's going well. I'm learning a lot. This summer I'm in a class about Milton. The professor has us say it this way (*Dramatically, pompously, raising one hand for effect*) Mil-ton.

**JANE**: Sounds brainy. (*Beat*) Sounds intelligent.

**CALVIN**: It is. But I try not to take it too seriously. You know, UMKC is just across the way. I could come visit you.

**JANE**: I've got a doctor.

**CALVIN**: I could be a doctor one day—Doctor of Philosophy.

**JANE**: Level nine English major.

**CALVIN**: Level nine. (*He takes her hand.*) You could come with me, come with me as I take that path.

**JANE**: I've got a doctor.

**CALVIN**: Can he know you like I know you? I've loved you a long time.

**JANE**: We have time. I'm young.

**CALVIN**: But he isn't.

**JANE**: Tell me another story or you have to go.

**CALVIN**: So last week I get a call when I'm in class. The teacher tells me to go; the police are on the phone. The policeman on the line says my car is illegally parked. It's in someone's driveway, and they can't get out. I say, "But I didn't drive today, officer." Someone had stolen my car and ditched it. I only had enough gas in the tank for them to get 20 blocks, and then they stopped. Most of the windows were broken, and there were these big rocks they'd used to smash open the windows on the floorboards. And 40s and cigar butts. After that, I started calling the cops "Lost and Found."

JANE: That is funny. Where's your car now?

CALVIN: Just out front. You should see it. The windows are fixed. I've got it all waxed up. The rocks are gone, and so are the bottles and cigarette butts. I could take you somewhere, just like old times. When do you get off?

JANE: At five.

CALVIN: That's just in a minute or two. I've almost told you stories until close. And look. My bag's full. Which story do you like best?

JANE: How about we wait and see. How about you tell me another sometime, and then I'll decide?

CALVIN: But what about Dr. Ryan Patrick Manfredson?

JANE: You mean me becoming Mrs. Dr. Ryan Patrick Manfredson? You didn't know I was lying? Here, have some juice before you pass out.

CALVIN: I guess it turns out your story was better than any of mine.

JANE: Oh my true stories are better than my lies.

CALVIN: Like the next time someone sits in this chair and tries to woo you, you'll tell them you have a doctor.

JANE: Maybe. If there is a next time. Let's go. It's five. But one thing.

CALVIN: What's that?

JANE: Now it's my turn to tell stories. And keep your eyes on my eyes when I tell them.

CALVIN: Honey, you can tell them to me all night.

(*Blackout*)

# Current Influences

## Musical:
Charlie "Bird" Parker, Chris Hazelton's Boogaloo 7 (*Soul Jazz Fridays*), John Coltrane (*Both Directions at Once: The Lost Album* and *Giant Steps*), Keith Jarrett ("U Dance"), Madeleine Peyroux (*Half the Perfect World*), Miles Davis, and Lisa Moritz (*Dream of Blue* and *Holding Time*), Jack DeJohnette, Rosanne Cash, Josh Ritter, Patty Griffin, Dollar Brand, Don Mumford, Brian Steever, Brandon Draper, Doug Auwarter, and Doug Talley.

## Literary:
Tracy K. Smith (*Wade in the Water*), Mary Karr (*Tropic of Squalor*), Stephen Karam (*The Humans*), Kevin Young (*Brown* and *Blue Laws*), Aimee Nezhukumatathil (*Oceanic*), Traci Brimhall (*Rookery*), Tasha Haas (*Certain Dawn, Inevitable Dawn* and *The Garden of Earthly Delights*), Chuck Haddix (*Bird: The Life and Music of Charlie Parker*), Ben Lerner (*The Topeka School*), Dale Carnegie (*How to Win Friends and Influence People*), Napoleon Hill (*How to Think and Grow Rich*), Ta-Nehisi Coates (*Black Panther*), *The Amazing Spider-Man* (Vol. 1, #302, July 1988).

# About the Author

Past Poet Laureate of Kansas (2017-2019) Kevin Rabas teaches at Emporia State University, where he leads the poetry and playwriting tracks and chairs the Department of English, Modern Languages, and Journalism. He has twelve other books, including *Lisa's Flying Electric Piano*, a Kansas Notable Book and Nelson Poetry Book Award winner. Rabas is the recipient of the Emporia State President's and Liberal Arts & Sciences Awards for Research and Creativity, and he is the winner of the Langston Hughes Award for Poetry. His plays have been performed across Kansas and on both coasts.

## Also Available from Kellogg Press

*Vacant Childhood*
Lindsey Bartlett

*He Watched and Took Note*
Curtis Becker

*Everything is Ephemera*
Dennis Etzel, Jr.

*Dirt Road*
Kerry Moyer

*Rust & Weeds*
Kerry Moyer

*I Love the Child*
Ronda Miller

*Winds of Time*
Ronda Miller

*Watch Your Head*
Kevin Rabas

Order online at kelloggpress.com/kellogg-store

www.ingramcontent.com/pod-product-compliance
Lightning Source LLC
Chambersburg PA
CBHW021409290426
44108CB00010B/453